A CAPRICORN IN OCTOBER

A COLLECTION OF THOUGHT AND RHYME

A CAPRICORN IN OCTOBER

A COLLECTION OF THOUGHT AND RHYME

DON ALAN GRIFFIN

PURPLE HEN
PRESS LLC

©2024 by Don Alan Griffin

All Rights Reserved. No portions of this book may be reproduced or transmitted in any form or by any means, electronic or mechanical, including photocopying and recording, or by any information storage or retrieval system without permission in writing from Purple Hen Press LLC or Don Alan Griffin.

ISBN: 979-8-9899630-2-7

Concepts, Illustrations, and Thoughts: Don Alan Griffin

Orders, Inquiries, and Correspondences should be addressed to :
Purple Hen Press LLC
P.O. Box 2793
Richmond, California 94802
(510) 778-0560
WWW.itsthedark.com
INFO@itsthedark.com

10 9 8 7 6 5 4 3 2 1

FOR PAT, DONNY, DANIEL, PATRICE, AND DAVID

Table of Contents

one.   Day 1- 11   1

two.   Day 12-21   21

three. Day 22-32   33

Acknowledgments   54

There is no rest for the wicked, the oppressed, or the gifted. Only the ignorant. ~ d.a. tha griffin

one

October Day 1- 11

#1
(seasoning)

Life is a trip, but I learned not to fall hard.
Springing up quick with intent. Never embrace scars.
Summa these tricks dismiss & wanna play god.
Above it, so I duck it. When tears season a dark heart.
Learned lessons from the blessings & the stressings.
The answers & the questions, the failures & the successes.
Old addresses. Same aggression. New perspective.
Tricky, how the shame game never resurrected.
Treaty, when the blame game never quite connected.
You can holla at a playa, if you really want suggestions.
I've been so much, to so many, for so long.
My backs dripping, 'cause these blades, are so long.
I'm back living, 'cause sunshine, is so strong.
It's thanks giving, I gave Griffin. They want more.
Can't listen, I told Griffin to hold on.
Life's missing, I love Griffin. He earned more.
With less friction & less distance. 'chu lie for?
I'm cross-crissing. The ex missing. They moved on.
The new mission, renew vision, and explore alone.

#2
The Shepard tells the sheep to watch for the wolves, but it's the shepherd who plans to eat them.

#3
Sometimes the right way may have the wrong signs. You can go any direction on a ONE WAY street. You just have to get out the car.
The law is for the car, not the driver.

#4
Life is too short to spend time blowing up balloons for a party that you ain't invited to.

#5
(i'm gonna grow)
Sugar beets, sunflower seeds, onions and a couple of avocado trees.
I'm gonna grow my food.
Castor beans, ginseng and a couple rows of those moringa leaves.
I'm gonna grow my medicine.
Roses, lilies, jasmine, & mint.
Sandalwood, lavender & lemon balm scent.
I'm gonna grow my fragrance.
Iris', orchids, & violets & poppies,
hibiscus in purple and cactus that copies.
I'm gonna grow my beauty.

Plowing & tilling, emptying, filling,
seeding & drilling, ready & willing.
Reaping & sowing.
I plant without knowing. I move without going.
And light without glowing.
I'm gonna grow my faith.

The smiles & frowns, the ups & downs,
the trials & crowns, the hate by the pounds.
The tricky situations that'll keep a soul bound.
Avoid confrontation enjoy days above ground.
I'm gonna grow my patience.

Deciduous breeds of oak, birch, and beech.
Ash, elm, and maple. Strength is what I need.
I'm gonna grow my home.

Sweeping then weeding, lifting then feeding,
patching when mending, and reaching while bending.
I'm gonna grow my body.

Sea moss & ginger, math book adventures.
Lion's Mane, mary jane, mushrooms may enter.
Blast off into cosmos then glide off, like I'm not lost.
There's a paid cost to be a true boss. Most stop before it pays off.
I'm gonna grow my mind.

I can cultivate my food, clothing, and shelter.
I can grow my mind, body, and soul.
My steps will be celebrated & anticipated.
But, my path still won't be lined with gold.
Character & facets are etched along this road.
Wearing scars as badges, a testament to those who grow.

#6
(darkxide, a song)

Sometimes I speak in we's, so the me's won't speak to us.
Sometimes I drop a need just to see who gone pick it up.
Sometimes I plant a seed & be surprised what bubbles up.
Look bitch, don't talk to me if you ain't talking about giving it up.
See, I'm coming from the darkxide. What'chu mean you ain't giving it up!

4 A Capricorn In October

This is my life and I'm gone fly.
we all playing games, but we choosing to duck.

See, I'm coming from the darkxide. What'chu men you ain't giving a fuck.
This is your life, why you don't try.
If you skip the game, you gone trip outta luck.

Sometimes I walk the street, so the street may walk with us.
Sometimes I drop a beat & see what kind of people pick it up.
Sometimes I'll walk it sleep. Just to see who gone wake me up.

Yes, I'm coming from the darkxide.
What'chu mean you're giving it up?!
You can choose life & you still die.
Don't quit the game unless you beating it up.
Yup, I'm coming from the darkxide.
What'cha mean you ready to go?
Life's a trip, if you just ride.
Good game'll have you ready to blow.

Sometimes I run with G's, so I won't get hung with ewes.
Sometimes the fonk I earn, is better than the funk I choose.
Sometimes the ones you love, will be the quickest ones to shoot.
Sometimes I wanna change, but ain't nobody gonna wear these boots.
I'm coming from the darkxide...

#7
Quite honestly, they'll call me brother when they need something and call me sucker when they don't get it.

#8
Life is too short to be waiting on buses you should be driving.

#9
(4:13, a story)

Sean has made this trip many times before. He calls it a money run. Hop on BART, get off, rob a couple folks, then hop back on wait a few stops and do the same thing again in another zip code. Not a very original idea, but he seems to think it was genius when he tells his buddies about it.

"Look! Look! Look!" Sean is obviously giddy about the idea, and can't wait to tell anyone who will listen. He's surrounded by a small group of what he thinks are his friends. Well, they are his friends in a way. It's just that when a person chooses thievery or strong arm robbery as a profession. No one really ever trusts them. 'Friends' are often uneasy, because anything they have could be gone from them, if the thief chooses.

"Dude, dude we listening, go on with your story." Rob says impatiently not really wanting to hear Sean's master plan for the hundredth time.

"OK, like I was saying!" Sean starts in and can't help smiling while he talks about himself and the master plan. "I get on BART in Richmond and transfer if I want to, then jump off hit the streets rob a couple folks then right back on BART before anybody knows shit. One day I got on rode all the way to Pittsburg ran down to that little strip mall robbed the pizza place and jumped right back on and rode straight to Embarcadero. In the city you know? Hella cops! I just turned around hopped back on and rode the bitch to Daly City. Caught the free shuttle to SF State got off at the mall, hit this Filipino dude and some young white broad. She had a iPod and a iPhone I-"

"See that's what I'm talking about you just say any gat damn shit. Why would the bitch have a iPod and a iPhone?" Slim says loudly. Who thinks anytime somebody says something good they have to be lying decides to interrupt at this time to voice his opinion.

6   A Capricorn In October

"Look I told her, gimme what you got and a iPhone, iPod, and seventy-five dollars popped out I didn't argue. I just darted back onto the SF State shuttle got on BART and came on home." Being question by Slim didn't sit too well with Sean he spoke slow to show his irritation with Slim, but didn't look at him on purpose. Because he really wasn't even talking to Slim. He was bragging to Rob. Slim just happen to be there.

"Aight nigga iPhone, iPod, and seventy-five bucks huh?" Slim's words are dripping sarcasm in big drops. "Whens the next money trip then Sean my man?" Slim intentionally called it the money trip instead of the money run as Sean called it. He's trying to antagonize Sean. Unfortunately, Slim has gotten what he wanted, Sean is very irritated as Slim is about to find out.

"Why I gotta lie Slim?" Sean steps close to Slim. Close enough where every breath that comes out of his snarling mouth makes Slim's eyes blink from the force of the words. "I don't like your tone Slim."

"C'mon Sean he don't mean shit by it you know that." Rob tries to defend Slim. Sean is listening to Rob, but hasn't taken one step back or stopped glaring at Slim.

"Well people should understand that when you shoot down someones hustle be ready to get shot at yourself." Sean smiles at his non victim, successfully scaring him was his only aim. For the icing on the cake he thumbs his .380 snub nose. Slim looks down quickly and just listens to Rob and Sean for the rest of the conversation. Sean broke him. Still intently staring at him too.

"Fuck all that shit cuz! Are you going on a run today? Is that why you talking about it? Rob interrupts the scene. He knows Sean won't kill Slim, but he may humiliate him. Robbing him, stripping him butt ass naked, and making him walk home is definitely in Sean's repertoire. He's done that before.

"Yeah, yeah later on today tho," still staring, and still all in Slim's face. Slim hasn't taken a step back and has looked everywhere, but at Sean the whole time. Totally intimidated.

"I heard the fair is in Pleasanton for three or four days gotta see how close it is to the BART tho."

"Naw don't touch that! In Pleasanton you already know they gone watch you from the moment you walk in till the second you walk out."

Finally taking his gaze off of Slim, "Naw, nope that's what I meant! Since everybody gone be at the fairgrounds I'll hit else where and be gone. You know!?"

"I gotcha, I gotcha, sounds like a plan my man." Rob beams with all the encouragement he can muster for such a silly plan, he'll be caught this time for sure. He's neither happy or sad about the outcome. You can't tell some dudes nothing gotta let them live and die on their own terms, he thinks.

"Well I'm up outta here! Watch that nigga!" Sean shouts, then points at Slim with his finger like a gun and shoots the pretend finger pistol at him. Slaps hands with Rob and takes off down the street toward Richmond BART.

Slim speaks to Rob only after Sean is down the street, "This dude lies so fuckin' much man! I hate niggas like that, then he wanna threaten folks when you question his lies. Ol' sucka ass mafucka!"

"Yeah? Well that 'sucka ass mafucka' was gonna whoop yo head if you kept talkin'."

"Fuck him I just stopped talking cuz that's yo boy and I ain't wanna get my cousin up here to kill that nigga!"

"Who, Lil' Sleepy?! Now who lying?"

"Hell yeah! Sleepy been whacking dudes since he was 13," going by what he had heard, not what he knew.

"OK Slim OK! Truth be told tho its best you didn't act up because Sean been smacking dudes about the same amount of time. I know of two dudes fa'sho he hit and one I ain't sho about, but I know he had something to do with it. The boy don't talk about the shit he just be about it. Forget about it Slim! It ain't worth getting anybody hit over." Really trying to inform the dude before he gets hurt.

"Maaan, Fuck him! He aimed his finger at me and pretended to shoot! That don't mean nothing!? Blowin' his stankin' ass breath all in my face!"

"Like I said it ain't worth it. If he really was gonna do something he wouldn't of said shit he woulda waited 'til you were by yourself and set your mind free. Believe that."

Relieved more than impressed by the tales of Sean's activities, Slim is still holding on to some false bravado.

"If you say so cuz. If he ain't trippin', I ain't trippin'. Nigga just need to stop lyin' 'round me tho cuz I'm gon' call'em on it."

Slim goes on and on the empty threats and macho bullshit start to sound like a bunch of mosquitoes buzzing, high pitch whining that gets Rob to thinking. Hearing the scared man talk, but not listening recognizing the fear and the "talk" that comes with it. The whole scene kinda tickles him, but he doesn't let it show because some men will lose their lives to prove a point. Cowards will kill just like a brave man would just for different reasons. Why risk it? Rob thinks if he can defuse the situation why not?

"Slim! Slim! Slim!" Rob pleaded irritably. "I feel you. It just ain't worth it. Quiet as kept the nigga just smoked some white bitch over $86.50 and a fake ass GUCCI watch. It was on the Channel 2 news about 2 months ago. Just cool it cuzzo."

Sean walks down the street trying to figure out where to go for this trip. What he told Rob was indeed the truth. He hit Pleasanton about 2 weeks ago. Too much risk heading to any of those anytime soon. He had hit west Oakland MacArthur area a month ago, not much around there except that florist and he barely made it back to BART. Well Fremont it is. Back to the top of the order already. Started this robbery spree 2 months ago in Fremont he figured he'd end it there too. Find another "big scheme" to exploit. He thought them Raider and Niner games are starting soon. He could clean up too, people act hella dumb in public nowadays. Drunks acting tough, like they're begging for it he figured. The short walk to BART was no more dangerous than any other day, but Sean felt strange. His .380 snub nose felt heavy on him it bounced against him off rhythm with the rest of his body.

Usually he felt as one with everything ready to run at a moments notice feeling free, not today though. The wind was still all day very unusual for Richmond being so close to the ocean. He just felt ill at ease. Attributing it to the run in with Slim.

Run in!? He thought, *Hardly that!* Sean sometimes speaks out loud when thoughts are too preposterous for his own mind. He is trying to convince himself when he does that. Kinda like it's easier to believe when you hear it out loud or even harder to believe. He laughed out loud as he thought about the look on Slim's face.

Sean thought, *that dudes been acting up ever since Lil Sleepy came back from the pen. What Slim doesn't know was that I was there when his cousin killed that dude from South-side. I told him if he didn't kill him I was gonna whack him. I told him I was counting to 3. I said 1 and he plugged the dude. I left and never spoke of the incident again. Sleepy is a sucka and Slim's putting all his hope on him. Ha! I should have Sleepy kill Slim that would be real devious. Ha! Fuck them niggas.*

Sean's mouth is smiling, but his eyes are seething. Real devious.

Sean made his way to the train and bought a twenty dollar ticket. Just in case there's a fast get away is needed, he didn't want to fish out correct change for a ticket. He made his way onto the train very little waiting at this time a day.

On the afternoon commute, everybody is tired and a lot of folks even sleep on the way home. Less aware witnesses in any case. He likes to sit in the two middle cars of the train. BART police who rarely patrol actual trains often enter at the head or the tail car. In the spirit of being efficient, they walk the train once and get off at the next station. Plenty of time for an observant person who doesn't want to be seen by police to hop off if need be.

Wow, Sean thought, *is today a holiday? There's hardly anybody on this bitch.*

"Or out in general for that matter," finishing his thought out loud, as he surveyed the train and platforms. "If I was a superstitious person I would take my ass back home, but my twins birthday are in a week and my mother's also. Ain't that some shit my son and daughter's birthday on the same day as my mother's. I can't forget that day if I tried. So, I must hustle others so I can show my love to others."

Something feels off about today tho, can't put my finger on it. I'll just ride to Fremont, hit that same watch place.

"Shiit! They had about $1500 in the register and I got about $600 bucks from those watches, quick sell equals less money, but all good. Anyway, two months later the thought of being robbed has worn off."

But unlikely.

"Should be easy pickings again." His way of reassurance was convincing himself that everybody other than him was weak and easily bullied. Under estimation is the quickest way to failure in most conflicts. Sean believes doubt is a weak trait and fights it all the time.

When in truth, a little doubt can make every move strong, if well thought out. He has doubts.

"I still have to be ready tho he may have a gun this time. That's what most folks do, get a gun and be hella scarred to use it when the time comes. Maaan! If he pull that shit I'll blow his mind Ha,Ha! Folk don't cooperate even with a gun in their face. I mean, I do regret some of the things that happen and the people I've hurt, but I gotta say I would do it all-

"Can you speak French?" A stranger asked.

"again," Sean finished his thought out loud. "What!? Can I what?" Sean was so deep in thought, this man sat down right in front of him and he never took notice of him.

"I think you heard me young man, but I will repeat it." The stranger paused, smiled at Sean, and repeated the question. "Can you speak French?" The stranger was polite with a melancholy tone. Like he was told to make conversation with someone. *Still odd question though*, Sean thought. He took his time to answer searching the mans face for insanity. The BART is filled with crazy people. The stranger seems normal, there is a look in his eyes that's familiar, but distant. Sean couldn't tell if there was a smirk on his lips or if it was just the way he held his mouth. He kept looking around. This is a classic set-up scenario. No one is watching at all.

"Naw man, I can't speak French at all."

"I thought I heard you say 'cosi buono'. That means 'that's so good' in French. I thought as much. I guess there aren't many black people who speak French fluently. *The stranger said he thought as much and that there aren't many blacks that can speak fluently.* Sean distinctly heard black people are stupid. Even though that is not what the stranger said. He wasn't offended, but he was defensive. Anybody that would talk about black people to a black person in public is either looking for trouble or off. And Sean decided that this stranger is off. This is the perfect seat, the perfect cover, and it's gonna be a a long trip to Fremont. He'll indulge the fool for awhile. Sean responded as coolly as he could manage with just being called stupid in his mind. "I saw on TV when the earthquake hit in Haiti all of those people spoke French."

"Yeah," the stranger remarked quickly. "But most of them are dead now."

"What's the fascination with blacks speaking French and dying?" Sean questioned the black hating stranger. In his mind, everything this stranger is saying is anti-black so far. When in reality he was just making conversation.

"Fascination? That's a big word and you used it correctly. Good job!" The stranger said with surprise lilting in his voice with not one bit of sarcasm.

Sean realizes this dude is either trying to get him mad or is just a nut. Either way the stranger isn't talking cynically, just matter of factually. So, he plays the game a little longer. Trying his best to be the exact opposite of every stereotype he can think of, meaning he can't get offended by ignorance.

"Well, fascination sounds like a third or fourth grade vocabulary word. Why would you compliment me on passing the third grade?"

The stranger smiles and narrows his eyes, delight dances in them at the answer Sean has given in reply. He said,"Touche! You are a-"

Sean held up his index finger. "Now that's French. Unlike the shit you said earlier that *cosi buono* sounds Italian. *Cest si bon* is French though for 'that's so good'. Anticipating the man's disbelief at this body of knowledge Sean explains," I watch a lot of food channel one of those food people says it a lot I think it's her catch phrase." Sean said all of this in his calmest voice copying the strangers tone.

"Well, well, well, as I was saying you are a very smart young man. You answered my question very well concisely and very respectfully even though my line of questions could be taken as disrespectful by a lesser man." The stranger boasts on Sean's behalf.

Sean is definitely stoking an attitude, but answers less calmly, "Yeah? Well, I would say thanks, but a lesser man would take that as some kinda admission of black ignorance. I ain't smart at all. I'm average for a black person." Sean didn't believe his own statement, because he in his own way thinks he's smarter than most people in general not just black. He just wasn't in the mood for a 45 minute conversation with a white man on the ignorance of black folk. He deflected the ignorance issue by sticking to his own agenda.

"And you ain't answered not one of my questions yet. And here's another one. What kind of person does that make you?"

"I apologize I did not mean to insult you in the least bit, but I do believe that you posses an above average intelligence than most blacks, excuse me most people in general." The stranger was honestly apologizing even though most of his statements were purposely loaded.

"What is this thing you have about black folks?" Sean questioned, from a place of rising irritation. And weary of concealing it. He used to play chess with his recently deceased father for hours. He never beat his father, but by his own choice. He would just enjoy the company knowing it wouldn't last for long. This conversation feels like a chess match. Strategic words well placed to stem the tide of the other mans assault of words. Sean was almost enjoying the conversation, you couldn't tell by his face though.

"Without going too deep into my own life story let's just say my life was drastically changed by a black person."

"Are we talking bad drastic or good drastic?"

"Very, very bad drastic."

"Well, I'm sorry to hear that, but we both know one person doesn't represent a whole race right?" Sean already knew the answer to the question. This man hadn't raised his voice at all. All though the things he said were kind of stereotypical, he hadn't been disrespectful to Sean at all.

"I do realize that. I also realize that some generalizations are true. I actually have a problem with the human race, the catalyst though was due to one black man."

"Are you gonna tell me what this situation was or do you want me to guess?"

"Ha! Ha! Ha! No, no you don't have to guess, but we can't start like this. Let me introduce myself. My name Is Steve Eisenberg. Former UC Berkeley counselor slash advisor, former husband of Monica Eisenberg, and former father of Denise Eisenberg." Eisenberg leans in to shake Sean's hand. His jacket flaps open and Sean sees two 9mms on either hip and the butt of another gun under his right arm.

A cop!? Sean thought, *I can sniff a damn cop out easily. He said he was a counselor though.* Sean without hesitation shakes his hands and smiles. Never giving any signs of knowing or seeing. That has held him well in his neighborhood, see everything say nothing.

"Nice to meet you Mr. Eisenberg my-"

"Please call me Steve." Steve interrupted, the first actual time he raised his voice.

"Nice to meet you Steve, my name is Sean."

"No, no it is my pleasure to meet you Sean.

As Sean repeats the name in his mind it sounds really familiar like he had just heard it recently. He still has 45 minutes to the train gets to Fremont. It'll probably come up in conversation. The fact that Eisenberg is carrying at least 3 loaded guns doesn't frighten Sean at all. He has his trusty .380 close at hand just in case this dude acts funny. He wouldn't even have to take it out of his pocket. Just shoot through his pullover. Sean is on alert, you can't tell by his face though.

"What's up with all formers in your intro?" Sean smiles trying to break the tension he feels because Steve has suddenly gotten very quiet and solemn. It probably isn't the best question to ask a solemn man, loaded up with fire power.

"My formers are all results of death and unfortunate incident borne from the catalyst I mentioned earlier," Steve whispered.

"Death!? I'm sorry I ain't mean nothin'. I was trying to keep the conv-"

"No, Sean how could you have known please don't apologize." Steve was changing a little his earlier mood had passed and he was getting sullen and sad. It was in his voice. Sean heard it well.

"I'm not trying to pry just ain't want to make you uncomfortable."

"I'm comfortable Sean. I have made peace with myself. It is a very painful cross to bear, but it will be over soon, the pain I mean." Steve gave a weak half-hearted smile.

"How will you stop pain? Oh shit! I think I get it."

"Do you Sean?"

Sean remembers the guns, the loss of wife, work and child. Its cliche and stereotypical to say, yet when some white people are faced with a hardship they take the easy way out. Taking as many people as they can with them. Sean is uneasy. He knows you only need one bullet to kill yourself. Eisenberg seems to have a small arsenal on him. He seems calm though, maybe he wants to be talked out of it. And maybe he knows who did this to him and he's on his way to kill them Sean decides to dig.

"Well I have two ideas really. One, is revenge on the wrong doers or the black catalyst. If you don't mind me calling him that." Sean reasoned.

"I have no idea who killed my wife, and I don't mind you calling him that if you don't mind me calling him that." Steve gave one of those half smiles again.

"Touche," Sean did not smile.

"And the second idea Sean."

"OK the second is kinda out there and very stereotypical."

"Oh, let's hear it nonetheless, I'm very curious."

"I was thinking you go somewhere public, shoot yourself and a few people. It's a stereotypical idea but as you said some generalizations are true. We are just talking hypothetically of course right?"

"Of course, of course hypothetically. You have, uh seen my guns then?"

"Yup, when you leaned in to shake hands I saw them then."

"Very observant!" Steve is smiling again, like when they had first spoke. "I said you had intelligence!"

"What do you mean HAD?" Sean leaned his head to one side with a sneer mixed with a smirk.

"Ha! Ha! Ha! No, no. Sean you are quite safe and very observant again. Although, I do believe I will kill everybody on this BART train, I will leave you to tell my story. You are quite safe." Steve sits back in his seat and watches Sean's reactions to the news.

Sean doesn't flinch an inch. He thinks about the people that are going to die. Realizing that he is in no danger. He leans back and searched Steve's face for any emotion. There was none. He looked serious, not angry just steadfast. He said what he meant and he meant what he said.

"Sean don't tell me a cat has your tongue."

"Naw, I was just thinking, if it was a waste of time to try and talk you out of what you got planned. I can see you're serious. No doubt in my mind.

And you really want to do this?"

"No, no Sean this is going to happen. It has to happen. They took from me. I'm going to take from them. I decided t-"

"OK, wait a minute let me get this shit straight. Everybody on this train is gonna die?"

"No, no Sean I have a two 9mms a full clip a piece, a .45 with 2 full clips, and a .380 snub nose revolver. With some quick math and wishful thinking. I think that's about sixty people. Well 59 people I need one for myself." Steve said thoughtfully.

"Gat damn! So when is this gonna happen?"

"Fremont station Richmond bound train leaves the station at 4:13 pm."

"Really got this down the minute, huh Eisenberg? Why so precise?"

"Sean, my wife was killed a few blocks from the BART station and have him on camera getting on the 4:13 train bound for Richmond. And Sean please call me Steve. My father used to call me Eisenberg. Well, my step father he was a very," shaking his head,"anyway, Steve please."

"OK, Steve I got you."

"So, any questions about the time I choose to die?"

"No I get it. Theory is, that the person that hurt your wife **could** be on the train."

"Exactly, and you're pretending not to be intelligent. Now I am a reasonable man and I realize the chances of the man that killed my wife being on that train at that particular time aren't entirely in my favor. But you know its worth a shot."

Sean narrowed his eyes at Steve and the two genuinely laughed out loud for a minute together.

"Very funny Eisen- sorry, Steve. Also very corny, but funn-" Not until that moment did Sean remember where he had heard that name

Eisenberg, in fact the last time he came to Fremont he robbed a lady and the name on her work ID was Eisenberg. Maureen Eisenberg no his wife's name was Monica. He remembers on channel 2 news him and Rob were laughing about it the day after.

"What's the matter Sean? You've been quiet?"

"Nothing I was just thinking."

"Thinking about what?" Steve whispered.

"What if you could kill the man who killed your wife? Would you still have to kill everyone on the 4:13 train."

"I don't know, I never thought about that."

"Well, think about it."

"Why?"

Sean thought, *Eisenberg said his wife's name was Monica, but the lady I robbed name* "was Maureen. Could I have done-." Sean whispered.

"What did you say!?" Yelled Steve.

"What? I didn't say anything."

"I never told you my wife's middle name you mumbled Maureen! Maureen!"

"Wait! Wait! Wait!" I was just thinki-"

Steve went for his gun and had it out very quick like he had practiced it. Sean pulled his gun just as quick. Both men stared at each other both with fingers on triggers. Pistols out stretched at each other...

The Beginning

#10
(pain)

I leaned in to pain twice, both times I was scared.

The first time was an accident the second time, prepared.

I did not hurt myself on purpose, but I was fully aware,

that the pain I felt & the pressure I pushed was in fact cutting my hand.

Now, the brain can put these thoughts in nooks & crannies away from

the pain, But the pain just salts and the aches will cook.

Curiosity crumbles from strain.

The reason I leaned into pain two times.

Was in hopes of trying to control it.

The dreams I believe & the costs I perceive, deceived.

I learned trying to hold it.

I cannot stop the pain, but I can stop the fear.

I cannot stop the swing, but I can stop the tear.

I cannot stop the rain, but I can wear the gear,

That'll keep me dry & safe from harm.

During the wetter times of year.

Fear ain't real, pain is though.

So to conquer pain.

I need to abstain.

And let all that fear talk go.

#11
(a conversation)

Them: You catch more flies with sugar than vinegar.

Me: Who's catching flies? That's disgusting.

Them: It means be sweeter and you will get what you want outta people.

Me: So, if I'm shitty to people I'll get more flies? Flies like shit not sweets.

Them: No flies, just be nice!!

Me: So, is the assignment flies or niceness?

Them: Forget it, forget it! Just get away from me.

Me: Since you're being shitty, I'm gonna go ahead and fly.

✺

Some people will preach a better way to be, but if they were so happy why are they bothering me?

two

October Day 12-21

#12
Anyone who plants hate, will never grow love.
Also, anyone who buries love, will only mourn it.
There is a difference between planting and burying.
Expectations...

#13
(the road)
The road of disappointment is paved with expectations,
self-serving favors, and the wildest allegations.
When blood is thicker than mud.
There's no need for compensation.
No need for retaliation.
Or outsiders in our conversations.
When water thats thinner than blood,
can come in and point direction.
Can kill, and say correction.
And good people, refuse inspection.
The lives of those neglected, aren't interested in who's elected.
Breaking the laws & jaws of all of y'all,
in hopes of being respected.

#14
Quite Honestly,

I've helped people I did not like. My goal in these situations were to be a resource that helped, not a resource that liked.

Meaning, I have to learn how to help, without my feelings clouding decisions on how much of my help they deserve. Now, I am judging not helping.

Resources, aid, programs, services, food, clothing, and shelter. All these things can be used against those in need, to leverage an action. A vote, a vaccine, a job, or even a crime. Those with access to resources will have an upper hand for those without that access. And some people prefer it that way.

So I help. With no expectation of repayment, acknowledgment, or judgment. Because it is not my responsibility to show others that good people exist, but it is my responsibility to be a good person.

Helping only those I like doesn't make me a better helper or a better person, it makes me a hypocrite. It also limits who I can help.

#15
Most of the people that like to putting people in their place.
Don't even have a place of their own.
Meaning, people that set people straight are usually the most crooked.

#16
I know people so consumed with other folks voices, that now they only hear those voices instead of their own.
We are being judged on social media, in courtrooms, and in conversations in heads everywhere we go. Good & bad.
Someone telling you how good you look is a judgment, a compliment.
We should be able to take all judgment perceived as "good" or "bad" without it upsetting our perspective. Our day.
I try not to take anything to heart, from people that don't know it.
Bee awesome, or buzz off. Life is too short to be unhappy.

#17

I used to walk into rooms with awesome people wondering, what was **I** doing there? It was because I was awesome too. It was very much the truth. But it is way too hard for me to say, even though I know I am awesome all the way to my marrow.

Having the right perspective will navigate you better than witty talk or extra money.

My meaning is, if you walk in a room & you think everybody hated you. Your perspective would be vastly different than if you thought everyone in this room wanted to see you do better. Jedi mind tricks because neither is true, unless you believe other wise.

Mind over matter, because matter don't move mines.

#18
(comfort)

Sometimes you have to give folks a reality check.
Comfortable is dangerous, no growth is comfortable.
The truth is uncomfortable. Getting stronger is uncomfortable.
You ain't doing nothin' if you're comfortable.
I hope this made you uncomfortable.
Get Busy! Create, congratulate, and conglomerate!

#19

I thought I could change them.
I doubt I can phase them.
Never planned to chase them.
Always planned to race them.
See, this life is abrasive.
The joys are evasive.
The pain is inexplicable, but the centrifugal is so persuasive.
Learning to love on the day shift.
Breaking the laws when the sun dips.
These fiends sell dreams & act out in scenes.
Then plead for heat from my cold lips.

> I know I can't change them.
> I know I can't save them.
> I know how to pick & choose.
> Pros far as sniffin' goes.
> I can give it, but can't take it.
> LOVE...

#20
(work before work, a story)

Wake me up!, Before you, go! go! Don't leave me hangin like a yo-.

Adam slams the clock radio, not ready to start the day, but knowing it really isn't up to him. He swings his legs over quickly onto the floor and winces a bit. The aching reminds him. Every morning it reminds. It reminds him of how his life had drastically changed.

Usually, he went to wake his daughter up, but today is different it's the first day of school and she's already up and humming in the bathroom. She does not know how much she is like her mother. He smiled, and went to start breakfast. Oatmeal and toast, breakfast of champions and poor people.

"Good Morning Deanna," as he passed.

"Morning daddy did you sleep good?" Just like her mother.

"I slept OK Cricket, kinda warm last night, huh?"

"Uhhh," the 8 year old pondered. " I didn't think so," she is her own person no doubt.

"OK, I'm about to make breakfast."

"Let me guess... oatmeal."

"You know it baby, hurry up I still have to comb your hair. So, wash your teeth & brush your face, I ironed your clothes last night and-"

"And made my lunch! I did all that other stuff I'll be getting dressed now Daddy." Just like her mother very independent.

Adam turned the burner on, the clicking echoed in the kitchen. Pot was already on the stove and full of water. He walked to the bathroom washed his face and brushed his teeth. Thinking of the day ahead, the week ahead, the year, this life. He will have to regroup. His daughter is all he has and the responsibility of that is overwhelming and deafening, in comparison to all the other "voices" in his life. Her life is the only one that matters. If he is willing to kill or die for her, shouldn't he be willing to live and grow for her. He will whole heartedly do just that.

He looked into the mirror spit and showed all 32 teeth to the mirror in a wide grin. He goes back to the stove, pours the oatmeal into the now boiling water. Stirs twice. Heads to the room to get dressed for his job, business casual. He remembers dressing way better than this in an almost dream like recollection of a past life. Like a movie really, but dwelling on the past is dangerous especially when you feel like your are so close to the edge. Any sharp edged memories will have him tumbling. He's lost so much and suffered so much.

"Daddy what'cha doing?" Deanna asked comically.

He had been standing in the mirror with his shirt on, shoes on all ready to go to work with no pants on.

"Nothing, nothing thinking about the work I have to do today and got turned around. C-ricket!"

"I don't know what that means still Daddy"

"OK, let's go to the kitchen get some oatmeal in you and I'll try to explain while I get your hair neat." He slipped his khaki pants over his shiny shoes and they both headed to the kitchen.

Adam fixed Deanna a bowl of breakfast with all of the things she likes, raisins, butter, milk, peaches, brown sugar, cinnamon, and blueberries. He no longer goes to the barbershop, just a bald head from the .99 cents store razor.

It costs a bit of money for 'Deanna's Oatmeal'. Obviously, she doesn't like oatmeal. He made his bowl with just oatmeal. Its just food, hunger sucks, and it will be greater later.

"C-ricket daddy?" She questioned, as she sat down between his legs holding her oatmeal wide eyed.

Adam grabbed a mouthful of oatmeal, one handful of blue magic, and a handful of hair. He took the comb and went down the middle of her head from forehead to the back of her neck.

"You love blue right?"

"Yeeeesss."

He tied the right side of her hair with a rubber band loosely to get it out the way, and started working on the left side.

"and I love red, right?"

"Uh,huh."

He brushed the hair from the front neatly into his hand then from the ear neatly, and from the back into his hand. Pigtails have never been that hard. He thought, *her hair is really growing and my wife never had a perm, so I feel her daughter should not have one either.*

"So there's an album that Roger left laying around, by these guys in L.A."

"Rapper music?"

"Yes ma'am."

Adam wrapped a blue 'knocker' around the base of her first pigtail wrapped three times and buckled the 'knocker' snugly.

"Blood & Crips Bangin' on Wax is the name of the album. The Blood side is red and the Crips side is blue."

"Like me and you Daddy red and blue?"

He split the pigtail into two equal parts combed each one and twisted them all the way to the end, opened a barrette wrapped the end of the pigtail around the back of the blue rabbit barrette, and snapped it.

"Yup like me and you, the red team calls the blue c-rickets as a playful like name." He continued.

"But, but what does the blue team call the red team when they're playin'?"

"Well, they call them slobs," he mused.

"I can't call you a slob daddy that doesn't sound nice. Do they like each other?"

"Yes and no, but what is important to remember is that they are different sides of the same coin. No one knows what they go through as 'team members', except each other. Like me and you. That's why I call you Cricket."

"Because we are the same coin?"

Adam turned his daughters head and repeated the pigtail process on the right side.

"Yup same coin, same team, and-"

She interrupted, "Same everything!"

Just like her mother.

Deanna had finished breakfast and stood up grabbed her bowl and took another mouthful before tossing both bowls into the sink.

"OK, Deanna we are leaving." Grabbing the Strawberry Shortcake lunchbox from the refrigerator and the Smurfette backpack from the closet. He told his daughter to spin around, checking for neatness.

She was first day of school fresh. A pink and blue pair of Chuck Taylors, with blue leggings, a pink tutu skirt, blue Miss Piggy shirt, and a short sleeve jean jacket. All chosen by her, fashioned after Cyndi Lauper 'Girls just wanna have fun' video, maybe. He opened the front door and she walked out and he made a quick check of the small apartment, making sure no lights or flames were left on.

"Daddy are we catching the bus?"

"Yes ma'am, I'm on my way!"

He knew what she was saying, ever since she received that Minnie Mouse wristwatch with the moving arms from her Uncle Brian, she updates him on certain times, she feels he should know about.

He locked the door and they headed down the street hand in hand. They walked briskly, because they were a bit behind schedule and if he missed the bus it would be 20 minutes before another one came by. She would still get to school on time, but work would be a whole other problem. As soon as the duo hit the corner the bus made the block. They turned to each other and said 'Perfect timing' at the same time and laughed at each other.

Adam helped his daughter up the first step of the bus steps. She could manage the rest and would let him know she could do it if he tried to help her. He climbed two steps and winced on the third, the life changing injury ached a bit, but went away quickly. His daughter likes to sit by the window and she found a seat to her liking, looking back for approval. Adam nodded and smiled while he dropped coins into the 72C's box, asked for a transfer, and smirked at his daughter as she was singing to herself as the bus driver printed him a transfer.

"Wha'chu singing D?"

"Karma, karma, karma, karma, karma, chameleon," she sang.

"You like that song huh? You know that's a man singing?"

"Duh, daddy, his name is Boy George," she smiled staring out the window and dancing on air.

"Yeah, that's right I didn't think of that. Do you know I learn from you sometimes?" Adam says things sometimes to 'test' his daughter. When he was growing up he saw parents take care of their kids physically, but mentally not so much. Children learn right from wrong from their parents, sure Sesame Street will do the old 'excuse me and thank you drills. But parents should really know what makes their children tick and what doesn't.

"You learn from me? What do you mean?"

"Yup, I think everybody has something to teach, even though they may not know it. No one knows everything, and anyone that acts like they do, be careful of them. Because they are acting, but you can learn from that also."

"Yeah, Phyllis said that Uncle Brian ain't about nothing. And he is about something, right daddy? Deanna reasoned.

"From what you know of your Uncle Brian, is he something?"

"Well, yes he gave me a watch, and he helps people that need it. And he has lotsa of money."

"OK, so what does that tell you about Phyllis?"

Deanna turned and looked at her father thoughtfully nodding.

"That she has bad information about Uncle Brian."

"Yup, that's a very good conclusion."

She smiled and was proud of her answers. Something outside caught her eye and she diverted her attention out the window. She was thinking as the bus passed Fuller Funerals stopped at the tracks opened its doors to look for a train coming, the door gushed closed and started over the tracks.

Deanna looks out the window and was in deeper thought, "Daddy were you thinking about Momma earlier, when you were looking in the mirror?"

She never looked away from the window, but she was studying his face in the reflection of the window. She is just like her mother. She saw him acting strange, but let the moment pass. Only to bring it up later, when he couldn't wriggle free. He could not tell her to go get her lunch, to go make sure her window was closed, or even go make sure daddy turned off the burner, nope on this bus at this time was the perfect time. He had no perfect answer. The truth is the only option. Is this too soon to tell her he misses her mother so much sometimes he wants to join her. Tell his beautiful daughter that, one time probably more, he had gotten so drunk that he fell asleep in the car. Very bad behavior, for a very broken man. If he tells his daughter these things she may become frightened or worse pity him, that is not what Adam wants his daughter to see when she see's him. She is the reason he has not drank a drop since. She is the reason he has not driven off a cliff or swallowed a bullet.

If he relayed this level of grieving to his daughter, but reinforced it by telling her how much his love for her has made him keep going in life would she comprehend it? Best to find out what she wants to know and tell her that.

Whatever she asks I will tell her. He thinks and croaked, "Yeah"

Deanna saw the pain in his face, and grimaced a bit. "Can we play the Mommy game?" His daughter said through smiling lips.

Adam smiled and hugged his daughter and said "Yeah," not as heavy, though.

"OK, OK, so would Mommy liiiiiiike, my outfit today?"

"Yes, I think she would."

"Daddy you're supposed to say why, remember?"

"Oh,yeah yeah I 'member. OK, your mother would love your outfit. Her favorite color was blue too. Your knockers match your shoes, which match the dress Miss Piggy is wearing on your shirt. Mommy would look at you and say, 'You Go Gurl' , and then she would high five you and snap her fingers."

Deanna was very tickled and beamed thinking her mother would have loved he outfit. Adam watched his daughter smile while looking out the window.

"That was a good one Daddy!"

Adam settled back and watched his daughter, his reason for living, his reason for getting up in the morning, and his reason for dealing with the hardships of his life. And he will always be there for her at any cost. As he rang the bell for the next stop. He felt thankful, but realized this life is not good enough for her.

As they got off the bus and started walking, Adam's daughter looked up the street toward her school and frowned. Adam noticed and didn't say anything. She looked back at her father stopped and waited and grasped his hand, and they walked together.

"Daddy does your foot hurt?" She asked as she looked up at him. He smiled and realized why she frowned. So much like her mother.

"No baby not right now, only when I run or go up steps. It can be a bit achy. If I rest it, I can keep going."

"I don't want you to be in pain, Daddy."

"Unfortunately, pain is part of life and it is hardly ever fair, but if you look at it right you will feel better about it." Deanna frowned again and rolled her eyes up as if thinking, and started to say something and stopped.

She walked a few steps and said slyly, "Daddy, what do you mean?"

"OK, some people see the bad in a situation first, like your cousin-"

"Rachel," Deanna broke in lightly annoyed.

"Yup, she gets a Barbie, she complains its not the one she wanted. She gets a bike and she complains about the color."

Deanna broke in again, "She gets a new pair of shoes and never wears them, because her daddy won't buy the matching shirt."

"Yup, and there are others who are thankful for everything they get. It's called perspective, its like an attitude. A bad perspective is like a pair of dirty glasses, it's hard to see the good, cuz there's dirt in the way. But, with clean glasses, you are allowed to see the truth. Life isn't fair, but setting goals, choosing to see the good in life, and fixin' the bad. You will see yourself and others as better people.

His daughter walked silently, as they arrived at the front gate of the school. She never looked up or commented just walked listening or thinking. Sometimes kids don't let on that they hear you. Adam really was talking to himself anyway. Life is harder than it should be and seeing the best picture will bring a better picture. You never know if she hears it from him today she may hear it tomorrow from another person and it will make sense. He is just trying to grow and good human being, he thought.

Adam bent over and kissed his daughter on the cheek and forehead. She smiled and started walking towards her friends.

"Have a good day at school, learn something and tell me about it when you get home."

She turned and waved started to turn back and stopped.

"I will keep my glasses clean!" She turned and ran to her friends who she hadn't seen most of the summer.

He thought, she is why I am what I am, and I must make something better for her. He watched his young daughter play for a minute, but he had to get to work. He was already tired, but proud & happy. Off to work.

"SIMMONS! I have never seen such lazy person you walk 'round here like you feet hurt and tired. If this not a good fit for you let us know! There are people who are begging to work here."

"Like your nephew?"

"Did you say something?"

"Yes, sir I said let me adjust my glasses."

"You don't wear glasses, Simmons!"

We all Do.

The Beginning...

#21
(NiftyFifty)

The truth of the matter is, I am finding it harder & harder to deal with things I do not care about. That goes for people, places, and things. There was a day that I said no to BS. I don't remember the day, but I do remember the weight that was lifted. I no longer had to pretend to have the patience for it. You maybe wondering what I'm referring to:

Gossip, I don't know nobody and don't nobody know me.
Sports, I tried to be an athlete, because my father admired athletes. When he died, so did my interest.
Pop Culture, I don't care what's hot anymore, just what's comfortable.
Relationships, I speak a truth from the heart and that usually turns people off, immediately. The truth only hurts, when you're living a lie.

Anyway you get the idea, the point was BS and my higher resistance to it. I was born on January 11, 1974. This year is the 50th year for me and black which means I am in the October of my life. You know, if life was 12 months I think I am in the October, early fall not in the winter, but I feel the cold coming.

It has taken me 50 years to get this independent. It has taken me 50 years to grow this much. 50 years of seeing how my world works for some and not for others. Accepting that reality and a bunch of other truths helped me see BS for BS. We should define our terms though. **BS** *is anything that is not directly attached to my happiness, health, or well being.* Now, BS may be different for you, but for me anything to deal with vanity is BS. Keeping up appearances for people who care about appearances. That is a responsibility. Arriving at 50 and getting an understanding of what I like and don't like *(excuse me I mean what is good for me and things that are bad for me)*, I have compiled a small, yet not comprehensive list of *NiftyFifty-isms*.

1. If you misunderstand me twice, you will not be allowed a third.
2. Don't expect me to treat you better than you treat me.

3. If I see you and you don't see me, you may not see me.

4. I don't trust people who complain about things they could change with less energy than it takes to complain everyday.

5. If your life is more work for me than it is for you, then I'll have to say, Adieu.

6. Give me a weeks notice if you need me, it'll take me that long to tell you I can't make it.

7. Nigga, I'm 50 my helping move days are over. I ain't carrying shit up no stairs and I think it's disrespectful for you to ask me.

8. If you only call me when you need something from me, I'll only answer when I'm in the mood for giving.

9. If the ugly truth hurts you, don't ask me any questions that may scar your pretty lies.

10. My love will no longer be measured in deeds. You gon' have to take my word for it.

11. My health & comfort is more important than your feelings about my food & shoes.

12. My intent is to elevate anyone in my orbit, who is making an effort to evolve, revolve, or dissolve.

13. If you've lied to me, then you've stolen from me.

14. Knowing me is a privileged that the entitled will never enjoy.

15. I always make my next step, my best step. That way I don't regret steps.

16. I offer opportunities, never charity.

17. I am scared of the unknown, but I do not fear it.

18. Once I have earned my peace, I will destroy anything to maintain it.

19. If I see you care more about your face than your name, I will give you 50ft. because I know you lack game.

20. My love isn't for the weak hearted.

21. Time is the only resource, I cannot hustle to get more of.

three

October Day 22-32

#22
(d.a.r.k.)

Defining Art Respect Knowledge.
Dirty Ass Richmond Kid.
Defeated Always Rebound Knack.
DeBergerac Aristotle Rodan Kierkegaard.
Disturbing All Remorseful Kings.
Duga Anansi Roog Kalunga.
Darkxide Axylum Recording Kompany.
Dagumba Apache Renshi Kindred.
Dreams Approaching Reality Kneeling.
Dalma Askari Rahisi Kundi.
Divine Arithmetic Ruler Kingdome.

∞

I am the dark and the dark is what I aspire to be.

#23
(eulogy)

It's not as simple as it seems to be a clown. People never really know where the paint ends and the blood begins. Maybe they don't care. Maybe entertainment is the main goal. After a real shitty week, who am I to deny them a laugh?

Anyway, we choose this job or responsibility; making people happy. Happy. What even is happy? Love? Hate? Sex?

We all have roles that were put on us. Despite our feelings about the person or situation it was still this unfinishable task of love which happens to be our job-role. Now, a clown may fall on purpose because some people like to see that. It gives them joy. A clown, may breathe life into an inanimate object & manipulate it into a number of shapes & fantasies and allow you take it with you. A clown may say jokes or a saying in a funny way, but always with a kernel of truth to it. Because that makes it relatable, makes it funny.

We are at your service.

There is a difference between a joker and a clown. I think all jokers are clowns but, not all clowns are jokers. A clown may care or not, but they are driven by duty this is my role. My responsibility to make people laugh. A Joker has learned that the world is the joke & he will only tell the truth about it. But he will present it as the clown would, only deep enough for those who are listening or other jokers in the audience.

I am at your service.

I am Griffin your clown for the evening. Hope you will enjoy the laughs I have prepared for you. Thank you, come again. Yuk, YUCK!

It's just that there will come a moment when you realize the person in front of you making you laugh is not a fool.

Now, anyone that tells the truth in a world of liars is a damn threat. But jokers are clowns at heart ,so they will play to one's vanity pride, or gluttony. With the turn of a phrase a *'know what I'm saying'* They will believe you're a clown.

Griffinstein was a clown. He tried to please people that never were pleased. Because people never are. He died from suffocation. He ran into a burning building to save people individually, that is exhausting. Do not cry for Griffinstein, he has already been reborn as D.A. Tha G.
Where Griffinstein suffocated D.A. Tha G. will be elevated.
Where Griffinstein struggled D.A. Tha G. will bubble.
Life is too short to be the butt of your own jokes.
Enter D.A. Tha Griffin. and Peace to Griffinstein.
(My Reason #8) Griffinstein's Eulogy

#24

(who do you think you are?)

I am nobody and everybody.
I'm the warm wind at midnight and the chilly breeze in noon sun.
I'm the eldest son of a dead man, with no stars or system to speak of.
I am the starwalker, the cold talker, the warm laughter, and the day stalker.
The fear lacker, the peer passer, the cheer chaser, and the backpacker.
I am the brother that will treat others like kinfolk.
I am also the kinfolk that will treat a brother like an "other".
I am the darkness that is in all light and the light that is in all darkness.
I am. I aim.
I am Him. He is Me.
I learn without being taught. I burn without being hot.
I earn without being bought & return without being caught.
I tell secrets, but you can trust me.
When I smell demons they do not touch me.
See innocence, but rush to judge me.
Hear, in a sense, but maybe that's just me.
I am disciplined, watch what I don't eat.

I am cinnamon. Spicy & still sweet.

I am a gentleman. But was raised in some rough streets.

Peaceful Violence is, the motto for this dark breed.

I am.

I aim.

I am Him.

He is Me.

#25

(fine line, a song)

Screams echo in my street, so I cock the 9. Fine Line. I must be doing wrong, cuz nothing I say is right. We singing the same song, should swing in the same fight. The pressure seems strong, but nothing can dim the light. Tell me, how can I be wrong if I know what I'm saying's right.

Never can tell when its my time to shine. I keep a heater in a cooler, but thats not the crime. Aiming to freeze a shooter, I'm pushing a cold line. Please Lord don't confuse'em. I'm having a hard time.

Screams echo in my streets, so I cock the 9, also in my sleep, so I can't recline. Put the stress on the beats, define God in every line. I'm not a product of the streets. I'm the equation of the design.

My mind slips & slides like the moon, wind, and tides. Heart pumping water tho, the pressures kinda high. My gut pushing sludge, processing what can't die. You be the judge I'm dripping a dark line.

Dark codes in dark mode for dark souls. Talk bold and most foes will just fold. Hoes choose to expose the bankroll, mob line now we know who to aim fo'.

Some people shoot first and don't recognize the crime. Some people see the thirst, then profit offa the dry. Some people seem worse & we believing the lie. When these people bomb first, AlHamDoAllah.

I put the poison & the remedy all in the same verse. They call it blasphemy, because my congregation is cursed. They tried to blast for me, cuz I'm making it all work. I shared the recipe, y'all sitting on the same perch.

Y'all lookin' sick to me, keep wearing this strange merch. Check the history buying worth ain't never work. Vultures & eagles, see ain't really the same birds. One eats you alive the other waits until you gone.

See, drivebys are mainlined by hot lies or cold truths. We heat tools that chop lives. We all fools, but these dudes with no rules. Will change sides then change back then change you.

I must be doing wrong, cuz nothing I say is right. We singing the same song, should swing in the same fight. The pressure seems strong, but nothing can dim the light. Tell me, how can I be wrong if I know what I'm saying's right.

Never can tell when its my time to shine. I keep a heater in a cooler, but thats not the crime. Aiming to freeze a shooter, I'm pushing a cold line. Please Lord don't confuse'em. I'm having a hard time.

Dark slang for the *Ring King*. Let'em drip, but they paid when the reign came. Don't trip, cuz we ain't from the same game. Don't miss cuz we aim.

Let the church say, Ay Mayne! I got eyes on you ninos, niggas calling foul, but I'm dunkin' all of my free throws. Arm cocking back aiming high in my street clothes. I don't have to pop you to stop you, check the "G" code.

How many times can I uncock the nine? Fo' these mafuckas decide I'm not God's design. Decide that my mind deserves to be slime in streets or the sheets where I tried to shine. So, I bang every time they color out the lines. Rather judged by my peers than hung out to dry.

Same thang, but the difference is, I choose the time. Tell me how many times can I uncock my nine?

#26
(deal of a lifetime, a story)

"Where is yo mama at?" Roger asked his son. Who was throwing Lego's on the floor like they were grenades and they exploded all over the floor with his Lego gun shooting his father.

"Pshrn, pshrn, pshrn!" Morris closed one eye aiming precisely, while tossing a Lego bomb over his head at his father.

"Boom!"

"Morris! Go sit yo narrow ass down!"

"Don't yell at that boy like that!" Aunt Parshell yelled.

"Tee Shell, this little bastards running around here blowing everything up and you know I got *shit to do to-night*." he yelled except the last four words he whispered.

"He is not a bastard, he has a father and it is you, even though you don't act like it."

"What?!" Roger smiled.

This is an argument he cannot win and he stopped trying after Morris was born about years ago tomorrow. He has been a bad father, but he was here, that should count for something. After basketball played out at that junior college Roger was trying to make ends meet, hustling and tussling to help his Aunt and his son.

"Tee-Tee everything I do is for y'all, you know I 'preciate you takin' me in and everything. I was hoping the basketball thing would work out, but-"

"Blah, blah, blah, you think you can talk your way of things by telling folks what hey wanna hear."

"I-", Roger tried to say something, but his aunt was on a roll.

"'scuse me what you THINK folks wanna hear, you are 23 years old," she started and held up her hand to silence Roger before he started.

"TWENTY THREE Roger, I know you have your own place and you trying to playhouse with that lil' girl you got, but I raised you better." He squirmed under her stare, even Morris was quiet. He had sat down quietly putting his bombs back together.

"Look Roger, I love you and I know I am no replacement for your mother. She is out there doing God knows what with God knows who for you know what. You are grown now, you will have to take responsibility for what you and Morris and that lil' girl does."

"Shayla," Roger said quickly.

"What?!"

"Her name is Shayla."

"Nigga, I know her motherfuckin' name! Now Morris knows I'm talking about HIS mother! Roger, you don't think sometimes and it worries me."

"Tee Shell you do not have to worry about me I'll make it work. Brian said he may be able to hook me up with a job on the docks out in Oakland, and one of the guys at work is talking about retiring, they will need another foreman. We'll be aight, Tee."

Roger lied. The truth of the matter is his high school friends Adam and Brian don't call that much because of basketball and school, and he was fired last weekend for selling a coworker an eight-ball and fifth of bammer weed. But he cannot tell her that, she already thinks he aint about shit this would just put the nail in the coffin, literally.

"OK, okaaay, Tee, I'm gonna take Morris to the park down the street so he can work off some of this energy."

Morris smiled and without a word ran to put his shoes and coat on. Parshell looked at Roger and squinted and shook her head. Seems like she was about to say something and took a breath to say something, but Roger knew more was coming.

"Huh, you need help? Here I come lil' boy!" He said to no one.

Roger walked into the room with Morris and just watched him putting his shoes on. Smiling, he saw his son having a hard time with his shoe, he was trying to force the shoe on without untying it and it was giving him problems.

"Man, when something is hard you have to look at it and find an easier way," he said softly.

"I can get it, its almost on." The shoe plunked on and Morris beamed. He reached for the other shoe.

"OK, for this one let's untie it and see how long it takes." His son shook his head, but went along with it and pulled the lace and stretched out the shoe, placed his foot in on the first try and pretended to tie up the shoe.

"Oh, nigga you think you slick, you don't know how to tie your shoe." Roger teased.

"I do, just not very good." Morris spoke loudly, but not yelling.

"Who you think you yelling at? Don't get mad at me because you don't know how to tie your shoe."

"I wasn't yelling, just saying," Morris sulked.

" I know yelling when I hear it!"

"Stop yelling at that boy, Roger!"

"He's yellin' at me."

"Nigga I can hear you!" His aunt bellowed up the hall.

"Are you ready?" Roger whispered loudly.

His son was still concentrating on his shoe game.

"Put your foot over here," he bent over to tie the shoe. *I need to get outta the house as soon as I can, 'fore Aunt Parshell come all the way back-*

"You should teach him how to tie his shoe himself."

"He should already know how to tie'em."

"Well, he doesn't."

Yes, I do. I-" Morris started.

"Boy stop lying."Aunt Parshell reprimanded sweetly.

"Aight let's go Morris." Roger urged, "To the park, baby boy."

Roger and Morris walked in silence, Roger thinking about how he was gonna pay bills and pay rent. He had small hustles going on, but slangin' bammer was more trouble than it was worth and that 8ball was the last of his coke. And he owes Geraldo $550 for that raggedy ass weed and the 7 grams of coke. Roger tried to get let a few guys hit the shit to get them to buy from him, but hits cost money and Geraldo had fronted him. No way to pay him, right now.

"Daddy can I go with you tonight?"

"Huh, yeah where you wanna go?"

"Uh, we can go anywhere?"

"Yup Chuck E. Cheese, Dave and Busters, the movies I think Toy Story is out."

"Oh,oh I know Disneyland!!!"

"Lit-tle nig-ga noooo." Roger sang, Morris laughed.

"Why nooot, you said anywhere."

Roger knew what this was about, you say one thing to Morris and he goes above what you say. Tell him to take a couple cookies he takes a handful. He's always been that way.

"You know we have to go local, we would have to drive to L.A. which is 6 hours a way, we would have to stay overnight, and stand in long lines. But I think you knew that. Any questions?"

"Yes, what is L.A.?" Morris smiled. Roger squinted and smiled and started to chase Morris toward the park.

"Boy, when I catch you, you gon' get it!"

Roger chased Morris. His son laughed loud and was very happy. The two ran up the small hill leading to the park. Roger caught Morris at the top of the hill and they rolled down the hill in each others arms. Once they stopped rolling, over Morris' shoulder Roger see's a group of guys sitting on the merry-go-round. He instantly recognized Geraldo and his cousin Pepper. And they both seen him after that tumble down the hill. He froze and started to shake his head, but Geraldo and Pepper started walking over to him. Roger grabbed Morris' hand and started walking toward the swings.

"You wanna swing first or monkey bars?"

"Swing!!! I like to swing!"

"You remember how to pump, right?"

"Yup I'll show you!" Morris yelled.

Gustavo and Pepper walked up behind him. He was watching his son swinging, intentionally not turning around even after he heard them come up.

"'Sup Rog?" Pepper sang annoyingly.

"Nothing much Pep whats up with it?" Roger stepped back because Pepper walked right up into his face.

"You know what's up? You owe money, brother."

"I know, I know, but I got fired trying to sell that shit and-"

"That shit ain't got shit to do with our shit, bro!"

"I know, G man listen I can pay you back I just have to get a job my boy is hooking me up fa'sho, fa'sho!"

"Gustavo ain't frontin none of that and we need that money right now, bro!"

"I know cuz, but-," Roger tried to explain again, was interrupted by Gustavo.

"Cuz if you KNOW every goddamn thing, what am I about to tell you to do?"

"Shit I don't know G, what do you want me to do? I can do it."

"OK, OK, I need you to go pick up a half kilo for me. To tell you the truth it's a quarter, the money is here." Gustavo spoke slowly, "Can you do that?" He pulled out a small paper bag that unrolled like it had a brick in it. Gustavo pulled out 11 crisp hundred dollar bills and handed them over to him. Roger looked and evaluated.

"Man, where do I buy this thing at? I mean I only owe you like $850," Roger questioned.

Pepper answered, "Do you have the $850, bro?" Roger says nothing just looks down and shakes his head like a child.

"I thought so bro."

"Daddy! See how high I am? Rogers son screamed.

"Yeah, I see you, that's very good dude!" Roger said enthusiastically, but looking squarely at Gustavo.

"Buy the coke and we even," Gustavo said. Roger shook his head yes and turned to look at his son.

"Yeah I got you G. Am I gonna get a piece of this sale to, I can rock up an ounce?"

"Sure bro, finish this first!" Pepper warned.

"I'll do it, I'll do it, where is it and when?"

"I'll call you bro, in about an hour."

"Pep stop calling me bro." Roger turned away from the group, "Morris lets hit it!" He thought, *I'm finally about to get the break I always deserved. With an ounce of coke he could get cracking and do his sons right and his aunt.* Morris jumped off the swing smiling and ran to his father's side. Roger held out his hand without looking and Morris took it.

"Answer the phone, bro!" Pepper yelled and shook his head. Roger raised his free hand and gave half of a peace sign, also without looking.

Roger's phone rang exactly at 7:11pm, he sent Morris home and hugged him told him he would see him in the morning.

"Hello?"

"Yeah the buy will happen at 10th Street park well lit and wide open in twenty minutes don't be late," the voice said without pause.

"No probl-"

CLICK

Roger was on Macdonald Ave at the BART station, if he walked fast he could get there with time to spare. After a brisk walk, the park came into view, no one was there yet. He slowed and thought about how he was gonna help everyone on the ounce turned into two and three keep re-upping. Finally, something is going right.

"Thank you God, a way out," he said out loud and smiled hard.

"You Roger?" A voice from behind asked. He whirled around answering at the same time. "Yeah, yeah that's me what's up?"

He saw a nondescript black man, maybe mixed with white or Mexican. Behind him were 4 or 5 guys behind him 2 looking at him and the other 3 looking the other way. Eyes in all directions so they can do the business.

"Nothings up blood, where's the money?"

"Its close, I wanted to make sure you had the stuff first."

"Blood, we been watching you since you left the BART station." The man watched Roger squirm. He did not smile, he did not taunt Roger. He did not like liars, though.

"Sorry, I just wanted this to go smoo-"

"So you lie to me!" The man was irritated, but Roger read angry.

"OK, OK don't get bent outta shape lets just do this, so we can be on our way."

"We will do what we came here to do when I say, not before, you lying to m-"

"I know, I know, I messed up, just lets make the exchange and go on with our lives."

"Now you are interrupting me," the man was visibly irritated. "Give me the money!"

"Give me the candy. I don't want any trouble. I'm doing a favor for G and Pep, what's all the hostility for, we're all trying to get paid right?" Roger, for the second time today found himself pleading.

"I'M HERE TO GET PAID. GIVE IT NOW." The man said slowly through his teeth in a loud whisper. The man snapped his finger and Roger felt the cold circle in his back.

He shook his head and whispered, "It's in my sock."

Somebody, not the holder of the gun lifted his pants legs and found the 11 bills neatly folded. Roger bolted. He heard 4 firecrackers explode and his legs stopped working, the concrete came to his face quickly. He thought about his sons, his aunt, and girlfriend. What will they do without him. He watched legs run past him, a car speed off, and a baby crying in the distance.

"I can't be dead, I have shit to do." He gasped. His head was swimming he could feel himself slipping almost like slipping under water he could only hear muffled screams and darkness. DAMN!

Beep...Beep...Beep. Muffled sounds from a woman and a child talking.

"He's a damn fool! Fired from his job, kicked out his house, and shot all in the same day. I'm too old for this!"

Beep...Beep...Beep.

"Sorry Tee 'shell."
"Boy, you ain't got nothing to apologize for, I'm just talking."

Beep...Beep...Beep.
"Baby Boyyyy," Roger croaked weakly.

Beginning...

#27

(for my safety)

If you under estimate a person, you're the only one who's gonna pay for it.
Learn what they are most afraid of and what they are most proud of.
Control it.
You will NEVER have a problem outta them again.

#28

(deserving)

Summers ending. And the love I tried to be cool about, is bitterly growing cold. The feelings, I was so sure about have all been put on hold.

The plans, I carefully ironed out, are creased, but still unfold. And the woman I thought I couldn't live without, has taken her couch and gone.

I deserve it. And she told me why, loudly over the phone. How it was impossible, to feel close to me. So she decided to give me some room.

Get The Patron. Get the fuck on. Forget the real problem. Create you a tomb. A place where the pain doesn't cut like a spoon. And it's okay, you're ensconced in gloom.

Time is a problem when dealing with wounds. Time doesn't solve them, it creeps & consumes. Time doesn't bother with the dreams of buffoons.

The crimes of the father you've perfected & used.

Time to get up or get down.

Choose.

Time is the rope, who's hanging out?
Noose.
This supposed to be love, without a doubt.
Fools.
Enveloped me, chewed and spit me out.
Deuce.
Sometimes the love you feel isn't the love you deal.

#29
(an abstract)

Dream   *Some*
Beau*tiful*
Vandals   **Memories**
Defend, **Prevent**
Revolution, **Dissolution**
Evolving   *Dissolving*
Purple   *Blue*
*Wel***come**

Lost in contrast.
Found in **the** rhythm.
Life cannot **last**.
The violence **lives** in'em.
Checks that **don't** cash.
Proclaim me a villain.
Look, but **just** laugh.
My look still **kill'em**.

#30
(knowing people)

Being observant should be listed as a superpower. Even if it's done half-assed, a person can seem clairvoyant.

What's funny is, some people do not see what they're doing as a crime until witnessing someone else committing it.

I know men that love women they'll never touch, and touch women they'll never love.

I know people who move away from trouble, but bring the problem with them.

If yo mama didn't play the Clark Sisters when she was cleaning up, your house is probably dirty right now!

If your life is more work for me than it is for you. We will have to deny your application for aid at this time, until you can provide proof of a mutual benefit.

I know people who are currently tip-toeing around people they should be actively stomping out.

I know people who fold their pizza & eat it like a taco. And people who unfold their taco, so it can be ate like a pizza.

If you find yourself defending your love, to your love. That may not be your love.

I know people who don't like my attitude, but its really my altitude & aptitude that's bothering them.

I know people who look, but don't see. Influence, but don't lead. Tired, but don't sleep. And cut, but don't bleed.

Some people don't play games, but will call you a king, treat you like a pawn, just to check your mates.

Some people will tell you they're above you thinking that will keep you under them.

I know people who prioritize the things they want to grow strong, and give no attention to things they want to weaken.

I know people who make shoes their priority instead of their feats.

Quite honestly, I only started practicing yoga so I could comfortably pat myself on the back.

You can tell what kind of person you're dealing with by how they appreciate things or depreciate them.

I know people who are entertained by trauma, educated by trauma, fed by trauma, and loved with trauma. But say they're not traumatized. Now, thats traumatic.

I know people who will tell a lie like it's the truth, and give you an excuse like that's the proof.

Let a lie live today. If anyone believes the lie, they don't know you and if they're telling the lie, they don't love you.
Pride is your problem, not these people.

A manipulators main aim is to make you think you need them as much as they are using you.

I know people whose words are cloudy, but their intentions are clear.

I know people who received criticism that wasn't constructive & in the spirit of excellence built with it anyway.

Quite honestly, at this age risking my freedom for anything other than my freedom is a waste of my freedom.

Quite honestly, if I tell you something about yourself, you can change. That's love. If I tell you something that you cannot change that is definitely hate.

I know people with sweet teeth. Meaning, they like sweets not that they posses awesome teeth.

I know people that slip into darkness and come out stronger every time. They are no longer afraid.

Some people are broken, some people can recognize this. They will never help you get better, because you are most useful sick.

If one of your friends eats with one of your enemies, you either have 2 friends or two enemies now.

Some people don't see life as a gift, because they don't live in the present.

I know I was told by both parents that fire was hot, but I didn't know what HOT was until I got burned.

I've realized that some of my opinions are just lies I've told myself, because I really don't like dealing with the truth. But, that's just my opinion.

#31

(the waterfront scene)

"I think somebody's on to what was happening. This is all too coincidental." After a long pause on the other end of the phone.

"I know I know that's what I-," A cracking noise interrupts the conversation.

"Hold on! Hold on! Something's not right." Damon pauses, "Ay! I'll call you back. Damon hangs up quick and pulls his gun. Sliding sideways into the shadows. He sees three men in black running toward him. They don't see him. Damon slinks into the corner ready to shoot as they run past.

Breathing heavy, "Eh! I just saw him right here did he see us?"

"Ain't no way he saw us. He round here somewhere. The second man cocks his glock, looking at the third man. "Let's merc this fool and get tha fuck on."

"Follow me, we gone check down by the water," the first man wheezed.

Damon snatches his phone and dials the phone, it goes straight to voicemail. Calls a second number, turning toward the waterfront making an effort to keep the men in front of him, he steps back making sure they're not close. Turns to run and bumps straight into Buck.

"Deeeee" Buck whispered, too loudly to be a whisper.

"Damn dude! I just called you!"

"Well, here I go, Whaz up D!"

"Ssh! There's some niggas down here to k- uh" Damon stops and looks at Buck suspiciously, "kill me," Damon finished.

"Sheeeit! We gone see 'bout that shit D!"

"I seen three but ther-," he pauses again. "Buck what are you doing down here?" Buck raises his gun quickly, too quick for Damon to react. Two shots ring out.

"What the fuck dude?" Damon spins around to see a man lying face down.

"Wha'chu mean!? Look, if these mafuckas is here to kill you then we gotta get them first right? Right D?

Damon nods, looking at the dead man. "Yeah, yeah."

"Well let's get at'em then D."

"Cuz! You really are crazy." Buck smiles. Damon holsters his police issue pistol and pulls his .45,"OK, I know they heard that! We gon' have to double back."

"We can get behind them, we gotta go D!"

"I'm ready," Damon whispered.

Damon and Buck dash toward the parking lot in an effort to get behind the assailants. As they thought the men are headed back up the hill toward the shots. Full chase now, Buck targets the slowest man and switches the gun to his left hand, freeing up his knockout hand. Buck with a well practiced swing punches the man in the back of the head he's knocked out in mid stride sleep in the air. Damon catches up.

"There may be more than three of'em I'm not sure how many we up against," Damon wheezed.

"Fuck! Don't trip D. I'ma head up around the otha side, they gone see that dude we killed. And prolly freak out."

"I'll get'em."

Buck runs back the way they came toward the parking lot and Damon heads up the hill to flush them toward Buck. Damon tears off. As soon as he sees the group he starts firing. Dropping one, the last two desperately search for cover......

Beginning

#32
(responsibility*bonus*)

If you wanna get rid of responsibility that ain't yours, stop accepting assignments from irresponsible people. In that time where they are "mad" at you, focus on that walk you need to go on or that closet you need to clean out. They'll be back.

Why?

Because you are the most responsible person they know. Now, when they offer you a way back into their life by giving you a task that will no doubt be full of fake drama.

You can say no.

And they will be forced to treat you differently.

Please remember, frame all of these conversations in love.

You are not angry, just tired of being stepped on by people who are supposed to love you. These irresponsible people may say 'You would do it if you loved me.'

Simply assure them that there will always be love. Do not prove it. Explain that the amount of love you have for them will no longer equate to an amount of work you will do for them.

Until you put yourself first, like you put others, you will always see happiness in others.

But rarely in the mirror.

END

Acknowledgments

I would like to acknowledge my family. They are my strength and my weakness, whether they know it or not.

I would like to acknowledge the people who have acknowledged me as family. I've met family at work, at summer camp, and just in life. I appreciate all of the people in my life. Some of them good for me and others not so much, but all people share lessons if you listen well enough.

I would like to acknowledge Richmond, California. A different Richmond chiseled me, raised me, scared me, and taught me. Funny thing is Richmond gave me the tools to survive, by trying to kill me. But the Richmond of today is the Richmond I needed. I appreciate the growth and the spirit of its artists, vendors, teachers, and streets in coming together in the name of Richmond's children. When we remove the stress & trauma these kids will blossom.

I would like to acknowledge my abilities. I hid from them for so long, because I was uncomfortable being me in front of people.
I am a philosopher.
I am a writer.
I am an artist, not an entertainer.
I am a student that will always teach.
I will never be done, I will always learn.
D.A. Griffin

www.ingramcontent.com/pod-product-compliance
Lightning Source LLC
Chambersburg PA
CBHW020810160426
43192CB00006B/512